Mzwandile is a writer who lives in KwaZulu-Natal, South Africa. Mzwandile enjoys reading and consuming media from a wide variety of genres; from academic to current affairs. Mzwandile's interest is in software development, he is a Google accredited Project Manager, with a focus on software projects, and he holds a Certificate in Machine Learning from Stanford University.

To the many generations of Africans, at home and in the diaspora.

Mzwandile Mbatha

THINGS COME TOGETHER

Critical Thinking and Dogmatic Indoctrination by an African Layman

AUSTIN MACAULEY PUBLISHERS™

LONDON • CAMBRIDGE • NEW YORK • SHARJAH

Ordering Information
Quantity sales: Special discounts are available on quantity purchases by corporations, associations, and others. For details, contact the publisher at the address below.

Publisher's Cataloguing-in-Publication data
Mbatha, Mzwandile
Things Come Together

ISBN 9798891555464 (Paperback)
ISBN 9798891555471 (Hardback)
ISBN 9798891555495 (ePub e-book)
ISBN 9798891555488 (Audiobook)

Library of Congress Control Number: 2024904385

www.austinmacauley.com/us

First Published 2024
Austin Macauley Publishers LLC
40 Wall Street, 33rd Floor, Suite 3302
New York, NY 10005
USA

mail-usa@austinmacauley.com
+1 (646) 5125767

A special thanks to my uncle, Mr. Patrick Khulekani Dlamini, may your generosity live for the ages through this work.

Tabe of Contents

Introduction	11
On the Sciences	12
On the Arts	16
On the Physical Part 1	19
On the Society	28
On the Physical Part 2	33
On the Politics	42
On the Economy	45
On the Psychology	48
On the Metaphysics	50
On the Religions	51
Conclusion	52

Introduction

The title of this work contains a direct and indirect paradox. The direct one, how critical thinking and dogma can be in the same title of the same book; suggesting some kind of coexistence between two principles which experts swear cannot coexist... Should it not perhaps be critical thinking versus dogma?

This leads us directly to the second, not so direct, paradox: by an African layman... Surely these are intricate subject matters... what business does a layman have talking about these things? Surely a professional scientist or philosopher has the authority on critical thinking matters, surely an ordained minister or priest has the authority on dogmatic indoctrination issues... what business does a layman have to talk to us about these things?

Well if you do want to know the answers to these questions and more then read on, you will definitely find this an interesting read.

But if, on the other hand, you find yourself questioning why, out of all laymen, it just had to be an African layman to address these issues, then the joke is on you.

On the Sciences

By the end of high schooling, some consider science to represent the epitome of human knowledge and achievement. We understand that this is because high school syllabuses around the world do make it as far as the teachings of Newton, and the world still is largely Newtonian in the way we see and understand existence. Looking around the modern physical built environment from the tallest skyscrapers to the fastest supercars, Newton's laws are sufficient to make these things possible. It is no wonder then that we take these laws, and the philosophical implications thereof, as the truth, for as humans, although we believe a lot of things we cannot see, what we do see we definitely believe.

But as we credit our achievements to the sciences, it is easy to overlook the achievements we as a people had made prior to the codification and application of the scientific method. We are now brought up to look at the world before the scientific method as a dark world riddled in fallacies. But in closer inspection of the whole history of homo-sapiens, we have to concede that these 'fallacies' are the very foundations that science itself came to be, they are the shoulders of giants that science stands on to peep further. We have to consider that, as humans, we still largely lead the same lives we led before science, just faster and more conveniently and for longer durations of time on average.

Science has been, and will continue to be, very useful, in cutting out the lies which were left over as a residue in human understanding while we were still using trial and error to forge ahead.

But, if science has taught us anything, it is that what we thought we knew in the past we actually did not know, therefore, what we think we know now even with the power which is science, future generations will prove we actually know very little, this is evident in the very history of science.

And as we do science, the art of scientific exploration has to improve. By being purists in these endeavors, we run the risk of stagnating the pace at which scientific discovery takes place. Now most scientists will see purism as an absolute necessity in order to maintain the quality, the integrity, and the stellar reputation of science. They see it absolutely imperative to maintain the original qualities of the scientific method. They remain very careful and prudent in documenting their discoveries. They remain very skeptical in their inquiries. They remain obsessed with rigorous referencing so that their work might be recognized by the community of science. And most scientists are convinced that they must do these things, that doing these things is in fact doing science.

As a result, science has become slow paced, boring, and riddled in jargon, making it inaccessible and unappealing to the masses. The resources that go into doing science, the way it is currently done, are huge, but the returns are either not relevant or not comparable. For example, one looks at the incredible feats science has achieved in space, and one wonders why a body of such brilliance cannot find solutions to the seemingly simple problems we face at home. The work of most scientists sits in libraries gaining dust until they are deemed obsolete by the work of few scientists. The few works which are chosen to proceed forward for the ages by the scientific community are chosen in a manner that resembles fashion.

As for the politics in science, it is counterproductive and has led to the many pseudo-scientific claims which rob science of its integrity. So, why then, with all these challenges do we continue to do science the way we do, clinging to the original ideas like an abused spouse who would rather tolerate the abuse in fear of the possibility of a new beginning?

In fear of losing quality, integrity, and reputation, science has headed in a direction where these things are being lost anyway... In fear of a possible regression to a state of understanding that was before science, we are pressing hard on the accelerator of scientific endeavor as we look straight ahead, we do not realize that the brake lights behind us are also on. In fear of the unknown, we are continuing our search for the unknown.

Africans, we must reignite a culture where scientists are encouraged to put forward bold new ideas without the fear of being ridiculed and being branded madmen or outcasts by the politics of the scientific community. We have to rethinking the issue of referencing as it is currently done. Firstly, because it assumes that a layman who is not well read cannot break the barriers of science, but just look at the things ordinary people have done that experts of the period had said cannot be done, we don't have to look further than the siblings who were the first to take flight in a plane, breaking new grounds in aviation and aeronautics. Secondly, as we have outlined it before, the history of science tells us how little previous generations of scientists knew and how little we know by the standards of future generations, so by insisting on referencing as it is currently done, we slow the progress of science, for we are using untruths to try and get to a truth; any programmer will tell you about the importance of using correct inputs, the phrase they use for this is 'garbage in garbage out'. A space must be created within science, where new discoveries can be made from a completely new frame of reference, a new paradigm, leaving the job of linking these discoveries to the greater body of science for later; in a way that is the definition of innovation and a movement from good to great science.

Africans, we even need to look at skepticism the way we currently apply it. While it has been useful in ridding science of dogma and even downright lies, we must move forward with the philosophical epistemological implications of scientific knowledge and not be stuck in Newtonian thought processes. Quantum theory is now over a century old, we are now even starting to see engineering applications of it. Quantum experiments have implied that at a certain level even the intensions and prior predictions of the scientist affects the results of the experiment; therefore, we must conclude that the religious application of skepticism as it is currently applied by scientists needs to be reassessed, for how many times must we have thought we are viewing the results of our experiments when in fact we are viewing ourselves.

Let it be known Africans, that some of the major problems we face will be solved by science. But this will depend on the technology we bring forth through these sciences. This technology need not be hi-tech at all, the usefulness to our people must be the only standard… we all know about the efforts and resources Americans went through to design a space pen when they could have used a pencil like the Russians. Not to say we must not innovate, we, more than anyone else, must design things using theories which are not yet proven if we are to thrive in this world… we must be so brutal in our engineering designs that our creations must provide the scientific proofs for the unproven.

In conclusion, Africans, we must encourage original research as early as possible. We must dismantle the bureaucracy which plagues the world of research by putting as much emphasis on original individual research as we do on working under an experienced researcher and suckling from their breasts the milk of good research methodology. Our endeavors must be as much theoretical as they are experimental, as much analysis as they are design. But most importantly, we must always be aware of the new scientific truths that our research yields; most important are the philosophical implications of our work, for these are truths that will become the reality of our future generations, these truths will be their medium in the same way water is to fish, that is indeed the biggest way that our sciences will redefine the status quo.

On the Arts

In each of us lies a cry. Should one remain introverted, this cry becomes less and less audible, and we are then forced to dance to the tune of the cries of others. But as we lock up our cry from within, it grows more restless and the cry becomes higher in volume and pitch. It won't stay inside, it has to come out. Should it do so involuntary it explodes and it roars haphazardly like a wild fire, burning everything in its path including ourselves. On the other hand, the voluntary transformation of what is inside of us into the outside, the expression of our being, that is art.

Art is the pursuit and perpetuation of beauty. But beauty is in the eye of the beholder and what is beautiful to one may be ugly to another, so it is in fact the search for one's own beauty, which is beautiful and ugly all at the same time.

Being so all encompassing, what then are we doing when we start speaking about what is art and what is not? What is good art and what is bad? We are simply trying to discredit the cries which are far removed from ourselves and promoting that which resonates with us. Art then becomes a rebellion; a way to scream no to what we feel destroys our point of view thus in turn destroying us. For somewhere in our being, we are always conscious of the fact that the cry inside of us is in fact us.

This is why we can say that art is power. It is the power that drives our thoughts and emotions, the power that drives our words and our actions. It fuels the passion without which nothing would be accomplished. It connects us and divides us, making it the basis for all communion and all wars. This is why we cannot ignore it.

Africans, the study of the arts is an art in itself. By refusing to take a point of view, leftist or rightist, insider or out… We run the risk of being accused of being on the fence, the worst kind of advocate, the kind that stands for nothing and falls for everything. But in fact we are being true to ourselves… for there is no ultimate fence, there is no center, we each have our own centers and that's what gives us identity. In the study of the arts, we choose to not be populists nor devil's advocates. We choose to remain objective even after study, for by being too quick to be vocal we become those students who spit out the wise sounding words of others for whatever reason, but then our own growth is then stifled. Let us take the time for our study to grow into understanding and our understanding to simmer into experience. When we start doing the arts more then we study them, then we are fit to be called artists; for the arts are about doing.

And as we master the art form, let us never stop being students. For the wise artist is the one who is aware of the infinite nature of what is still to be learned compared to what has already been mastered.

Art is about imagination. How far can we go exactly? We can go as far as our wildest dreams, from the heights of the mind to the depths of the emotions. But Africans, let us not make this the essence of our art. Let us not be fake deep, always seeking the shock factor while the art itself becomes weak and tasteless. Not to say our art must be limited to certain boundaries, never, then it would not be art… But when we try too hard, when we are not being true to ourselves, this too would not be art, and the trained eye will be able to tell.

We are told that for the Africans of old, art was not just leisure or a hobby, but an integral part of life. To the ancestors, may they rest in peace, art formed part of their religion. A totem pole was more than just a record of history as many of us think of it today… When sculpted before the generations that are carved on it, it was in fact a prayer, which in the process of being fulfilled would become a prophecy.

This is possible because art is creativity, a way for simple and complex forms to crystallize into the physical from the heights of the mind and the depths of the heart.

And today, even as the arts have been relegated to the fringes of the center of society, let us not underestimate its importance. For even today, in this product orientated commercial world, the factory that produces a product would close down, and all the executives, all the engineers and scientists and all the technical and general staff would be laid off and the product decommissioned if it was not for the conceptualizers, the copyrighters, the graphic designers, the film makers, models and actors who have to convince the public that they need that product.

This is why art is not yet at the fringes of society but at the fringes of the center of society. This is why art, like knowledge, still is power; and why we must take our time with the mastery thereof. We must take our time with the mastery of the techniques of our art, and then develop new, refined techniques. We must take our time with the mastery of the craft of our art through study, apprenticeship, the discovery of self and whatever other means necessary.

But let us remember that art is influenced by culture and at the same time art influences culture. Being aware of this perpetual cycle will perhaps be even more important than even the products we sell using our art. For the cultures we create through the arts will be the medium in which our future generations shall reside, like the sky is to the birds.

Ultimately, when our art encompasses all knowledge that we cannot differentiate it from science, when we reach the highest level of technicality and craftsmanship, but at the same time break new grounds in creativity... Then the arts will reclaim the glory of old and usher in an era where truth will be beauty and beauty will be truth.

On the Physical Part 1

As a child, one imagines the world and the universe as they see it. There is the earth (dirt) which is down and the sky which is up. The sun, the moon, the clouds and the stars are all in the sky (and sometimes an aircraft or birds) while everything else is on the ground…

As one grows up, perhaps the thoughts expand, for example… if observant a child might conclude that since the clouds sometimes cover the sun but the sun is never in front of the clouds, then the sun must be further away than the clouds. Now this conclusion might be taken for granted by most, but it is a child's first insight into the concept of the sky having depth, and not just a flat disc with all these things stuck on it and moving about. A simple observation one might think, but one will be surprised how many adults are struggling with such concepts, who have never (or have forgotten) making such inquiries in their own lives. These are unfortunately the adults who make this world an unnecessarily hard place to reside in.

Don't get this wrong, this is not to say uneducated people are causing all the problems, no, to the contrary. The main disturbers of the peace have quite a large number of educated and uneducated people alike. Education doesn't seem to be a contributing factor when determining whether one will leave this world a better place to live in than they found it. For example, one might go to school and be told the earth is actually round like a ball and not flat, and one might actually believe this as a fact, they have now been educated. But if one simply believes this because they are told, then they are part of the problematic people we speak of. If, on the other hand, one is able to formulate some kind of reasonable explanation as to why the world is ball shaped to themselves through observation or logic, then that person, educated or not, is a critical thinker.

What this means is that although they have been told about the roundish nature of the earth, they kept the possibility that this might not be true, until they proved it to themselves without a doubt… Maybe by observing how a ship disappears on the horizon the same way a small toy car would disappear if a child was to play with it by driving it across to the other side of a basketball... Maybe by understanding why an aircraft flying at altitude in one direction, say eastwards, will eventually return to the same location approaching from the west. Again, such things most people take as trivial fact, but there are still people from some parts of the world who will tell you that you are lying if you told them such a thing, who would argue with you even before you give them an explanation or demonstration, who would even refuse to hear an explanation and accuse you of blasphemy, brainwash or worse for even attempting to sway their world view. But even worse, if gifted in persuasion and are in a position of influence... they would worst of all lead others into the pits of their ignorance.

The ancestors, may they rest in peace, were far more inquisitive about both the physical and nonphysical world than we are. It is said that the elders thought for long, a long time ago, and observed that since everything falls to the earth, how come the sun stays up in the sky and does not fall... They concluded that there must be an invisible pedestal keeping it up, they called it by many names, the force which keeps the sun up, the magic which keeps the sun up, the god of the sun driving it on a chariot, and so on. The elders then did the same thing with the moon, the clouds and the stars in the night sky. They realized that when there were no clouds it did not rain and if it did not rain there are no crops to eat and waters to drink... And so the elders marveled at and worshiped the rain gods and goddesses of old, and begged them never to unleash the wrath of no-rain which will lead to thirst and starvation... And as the elders continued to observe, they saw that the crops in the shade did not grow as much as those in the sun, and concluded that the crops must suckle from the sun goodness in a similar way a baby suckles the goodness of milk from its mothers breasts and therefore we who consume these crops consume the goodness of the heavens, and so they marveled at and worshiped the sun.

Today we have fancier names then magic and gods to explain things... At an early age we learn about precipitation which forms clouds thus giving us water; and photosynthesis which the sun provides for the plants to grow. We know a whole lot more about the world and universe, at schools we have been asked to build miniature volcanoes and solar systems and explain how they work... We want to dwell on the history of how we came to know these things, and why everyone needs to know these things regardless if they will have a career in the sciences or not.

The physical world gives us a glimpse at how things work in general, and we can apply this knowledge in all facets of life and living. For we have observed that in existence, things that happen are similar to or can be compared to other things that happen. This concept has been known in the east for a long time, thus generations of people who dedicated their lives to figuring out the way of things… how things work, in general. For example, Lau Tzu; who said that the great way of things is like the ocean, which becomes king to all rivers and streams by remaining low and humble allowing them to flow to it. This is a profound statement touching on matters of geography (the topology of the earth), physics (gravity and fluid mechanics), psychology (the importance of humility as a personality trait) and politics (the importance of humility and service from leaders to the people). Today, the globalized community has the gift of science, where the workings of some things are not just speculation, but proven natural laws which are facts under given conditions. But the knowledge has become so vast, we have been forced to specialize, leaving little to no time in stringing the entire body of knowledge together… Thus one struggles to find generalized wisdom comparable to that of Lau Tzu. Ironically, Lau Tzu himself predicted this would happen, he warned that the many names that we give to things will eventually confuse us; he said that the great way of things is both named and un-named at the same time… when unnamed we are able to see its deep underlying mysteries… when named, the many names we have today, we only see the manifestations… we only see that which is in front of us. Knowing what we know now, one wonders if master Tzu knew back then how right he was.

Like humans, human knowledge started in Africa. From tool manufacturing, to the burying of the dead in religious ceremony, to visual arts such as rock painting and sculpture to music and language to the knowledge of plants, animals, terrain and weather patterns. The center of human knowledge would eventually leave Africa… but since things are, generally speaking, returning, it is a reasonable inference that the center of knowledge will one day return to Africa. When the Greeks took over the torch and continued the work of African scholars, Africa already had the knowledge that would go on to build complex societies and cities as north as Cairo and as south as Zimbabwe. From farming to metallurgy, geometry and land surveying, stone masonry and construction methods, Africa had already made advancements in the law such as codification and the jury system and in religion by formalizing it and building temples of worship, in education through the mystery schools and had developed knowledge systems that preceded the sciences, like astrology which would lead to astronomy and alchemy which would lead to chemistry.

African scholarship would eventually succumb to dogma and war… from internal conflicts (like Kush vs. Kemit) to the Persian invasion, to the Greek invasion, later the Romans, then the Arabs, and much later the French and British colonial occupation… African scholars fled and scattered all over Africa hiding in the caves of the highest mountains and deepest valleys, living obscure lives secluded from society, appearing only as advisers to the people who sought their council. Their brotherhoods were infiltrated by charlatans. African knowledge systems were either lost or pushed deep underground, even outlawed and branded as witchcraft by those who did not know it in their arrogance, ignorance or both.

The Greeks inherited from African mystery schools a number system which was theoretical rather than practical. Rather than putting emphasis on calculations, they dwelt more on the properties of numbers. Pythagoras and his students are said to have believed in the magical powers of numbers, they believed the world is ultimately created in numbers. They failed to move from numerology towards serious arithmetic because of the Greek system of numerical notation, the way they wrote their numbers was simply not good, making computation near impossible. The geometry that the Greek scholars inherited was quite extensive and had been used for practical applications in Africa in the fields of land surveying and architecture for many years before. But what the Greeks did which was amazing and would lead to science as we know it was introduce the notion of proofs, when Themes set out to show that one can conclude a premise to be true using pure reason by using earlier known premises… Euclid developed hundreds of theorems from just ten assumptions, his work is still taught in schools today. When Alexandra the Great conquered parts of Africa, Greek scholars and Africans scholars would once again meet up. The works that Alexandrians like Archimedes and Hipparchus did back on African soil was so advanced that medieval scholars a thousand five hundred years later simply picked up where they left off.

Science suffered during the Roman times… Politics, war, and dogma became the order of the day. This would continue through the medieval times in Europe where even bathing more than once a month was frowned upon as an aristocratic exercise left by the Roman colonizers. The crusades saw people go to war in faraway lands to spread and uphold their dogmata... It was 'believe or die' in those days, leaving very little for scientific thought processes of inquiry. The Protestants were the first to rebel against the authorities of the time, but they too were not willing to take it all the way and do away with dogma, their own dogmata would see them burn people in extreme cruelty who they believed to be witches. If you had a quarrel with someone and they accused you of being a witch, you were burnt. If your baby had a birthmark and you were accused of being a witch, you were burnt. If you did things differently, you were burnt. Hundreds of thousands of people must have perished in the crusades and witch hunts. The renaissance brought the beginning of the end to this sad period in human history. Suddenly every curious person could delve into the study of their choosing, from anatomy to black magic. Suddenly a lot of interest was back into subject matters that the Greek had been busy with more than a millennium and a half ago.

Copernicus would be one of the first scholars to go against the teachings of Aristotle and Ptolemy which had been endorsed by church leaders. Copernicus suggested that the earth was not the center of the universe and that it actually revolved around the sun, the so called heliocentric view. This is at a time when people who said such things were murdered by the authorities for going against their dogma. For the church authorities, it was important that the earth be the center of everything for it reinforced the self-righteous idea that we are special and unlike anything else in the universe. Kepler, a student of Copernicus would go on to show that not only is the Sun the center of the solar system, but would use mathematics to show that the planets were following elliptical orbits rather than perfect circles as believed by the Greek scholars of old. Mathematics could now be used by western scholars, for the Moors, who had controlled southern Europe had brought with them the Arabic number system which we still use today and which had originated in India. This was the start of true science as we know it today taking shape.

This innovation would be continued by Galileo Galilee, who on top of using mathematics had developed a culture of observation. Had the Greeks been a little bit more observant, they would have noticed that a lot of their theories simply were not true, like stating that projectiles travel horizontally before dropping vertically and that heavier objects fall faster than lighter objects. Galileo took this obsession with observing to the next level adding the contribution of experimentation to science as we know it today. He would climb the Leaning Tower of Pisa and show that objects of different masses would reach the ground at the same time if you ignore the effects of air friction (a flat piece of paper for example would fall slower because of rubbing against the air) and ignore the effects of buoyancy (the tendency to float, for example a balloon filled with air is more buoyant than a balloon filled with water and thus falls slower). Galileo, using designs from another scholar would build his own telescope and look at the night sky. He came to adopt the heliocentric view, but was forced by church authorities to recant his findings publicly or face execution. Galileo also developed the principle of inertia. The Greek had believed that for an object to move there had to be a force driving it, but it was shown that this was not true and that moving objects had a momentum even after a force stops pushing them.

These innovators were changing the way people see the universe. Descartes would develop mechanical philosophy, where the universe was thought of as a complicated machine whose workings could be determined. The first principle of mechanical theory was the no action from a distance principle… that things, in order to affect each other, must be near each other. Other aspects of mechanical thought were absolute time, that an hour here is an hour everywhere, and absolute space, that here and there are two different places separated by at least a straight line which gives us the shortest distance from here to there. The mechanical world view became widely accepted by scholars of the period, all that was short was the mathematics which was weak and could not explain some of the things that were being observed. Descartes himself would develop the Cartesian plain by adding the x and y axes to geometrical objects giving them coordinates, what we call analytical geometry, paving the way for such things as modern GPS systems to be possible. By adding the third z-axis, one could just as easily work with three dimensional geometries. But the biggest innovation mathematically was to come from Newton with his calculus.

It is hard to imagine doing physics or mathematics today without the processes of integration and differentiation and other operations which are synonymous with calculus. In fact, calculus is today afforded as much respect as algebra in mathematics and is central to applied mathematics. Newton then decided to study motion. He proposed that the same force that causes an apple to fall from a tree is possibly the same force that keeps the planets and moons moving the way they do, the force of gravity. Newton concluded that all objects containing a mass attract each other with the force of gravity, and that this force was directly proportional (it increases) to the product of their masses, and inversely proportional (it decreases) to the distance squared between their center of masses... In other words, the heavier the objects are and the closer they are together, the more they attract each other with this force gravity. This is a bold statement since it goes against the first principle of mechanical theory, for it suggests that things that are not touching, not connected, far away from each other were in fact affecting each other. From this, mathematics and experimentation, Newton was to find that he was correct about the basic nature of this force gravity, and would go on to develop the three laws of motion; that objects remain stationary or moving at the same speed and direction, unless a force acts on them; that the force acting on objects is given by how fast their momentum is changing; and lastly that for every action there is an equal and opposite reaction.

As they say, the rest is history. Newton's work can be considered as revolutionary, for it not only revolutionized mathematics and physics, but science in general. Philosophically, it cemented determinism (that the secrets of nature can be figured out) and causality (that things that happen are caused by something). At first, scientists thought empiricism was the way, that they just needed to collect as much data as they could and analyzing it would reveal the secretes of nature. Soon they realized that this was too slow, and that they should rather collect data to test certain hypotheses they had formulated. And finally, there it was; the scientific method. Hypotheses, experimentation, mathematics, analysis, conclusions... Soon, new scientific breakthroughs would lead to new technologies; new technologies meant better ways to apply the scientific method thus new scientific discoveries. This chain reaction would go on to see the industrial revolution; new technologies from steam engines to the internal combustion engines we see in cars today. Even breakthroughs in medicine such as the development of germ theory that would lead to cleaner hospitals and homes saving millions of lives, even these can be credited to the pioneers of the scientific revolution.

Things continued smoothly for two hundred odd years. Scientists became the new authority on truth. A lot of questions were answered, and those that were not answered were taken care of by a rich atmosphere of scientific optimism, that they shall soon be answered. Soon Maxwell had combined electricity and magnetism, in a way which seemed to explain the whole physical spectrum of phenomena, making all the electric gadgets and computer technologies we see today theoretically possible.

Today, the world of Newtonian thought processes persist. A lot of scientists are happy to call themselves atheists without the fear of being put to death. A lot of people say science is their religion; that they believe in science, whatever that means… It is important to note that Newton himself was a devout religious man; if you were to ask him where he found the inspiration to do the work he did he would tell you from God. Newton, like many scholars from that time, was not necessarily just a scientist, a mathematician or even a philosopher… If you had to ask him, he was more an alchemist, a black magician. In those days, in the same way leaders consult scientists for advice in today's informed democracies, back then leaders would go to the likes of Newton for advice, wise men, who would gladly advise them not using statistics, but using astrology, the zodiac system, the position of the stars and how that relates to cycles of nature, the cycles of the kingdom and the cycles of the personal life of the rulers themselves. They would use numerology and all these knowledge systems we reject today as pseudoscientific and downright lies… And yet leaders continued to seek advice from the wise men of old, their advice must have been of some quality.

Newton was a theist, a believer… Many of his experiments, perhaps never published, were in pursuit of God. To honor Newton, the church ordained him, for surely a man given such insights into the workings of nature must be a man of God, the church thought… And so Newton was even a priest… And when he died he was buried inside a church… Future generations of his faith will probably declare him a saint in death as he was knighted a sir in life; and they shall see him in the same light as he saw St. Paul and St. Peter.

As for the sciences, although physics has gone through another revolution a century ago, it is unclear whether the rest of the sciences have followed suit. Science is still largely empirical. Further, science is now an established body, making it susceptible to its own politics, its own norms… its own dogma so to say. But more than this, the profit motive coupled with other social and economic norms means that science will only continue to thrive if to do so will result in money. Investments in science and technology will result in a loss for investors if the technology derived from that science is decentralized, if it is widely available and easy to replicate. This means that science for the sake of science is currently dead.

With all the challenges of social, political and economic nature, science will surely over time overcome these, surely. For science, out of all the established bodies, remains the only one that retains falsifiability at its core. This means that any serious scientist, rather than claiming the truth, reserves the possibility that they can be proven wrong, in fact they dare you to prove them wrong.

As for the philosophical epistemological implications of science, that remains the most important contribution and legacy that science will leave for the future generations. For the laws of nature we deduce, how things work in general, those are the truths that our children will use as foundations to build better societies.

On the Society

So far, we have spoken about the sciences and then the arts. And then we spoke about our understanding of the physical, and now we are about to speak about our understanding of society. If you are a critical thinker, you are starting to notice a pattern. You have noticed how we flip flop from a left brain based type knowledge system to a right brain type knowledge system and vice versa. The duality observed in the title of this work, this interaction between critical thought and dogma seems to be a continuous theme. And yet still, things are coming together. So what is this sorcery we are conducting on you, shaking you from side to side in the realms of the mind?

The ancestors, may they rest in peace, spent many years doing the exact same exercise we are busy with here. In the mystery schools of old, the students would spend many years at the left eye school (the left eye is connected to the intuitive right brain) followed by many years at the right eye school (logical left brain) before graduating as a priest. The priest, back in those days, was not a priest as we think of one today, a theological expert, no. The priest was more like today's professors, but instead of having PhDs in a single subject, they were experts in all subjects of the day, from physics to medicine right through to theology.

Today, we live in a society where one is expected to specialize in a single field of study. We are thus faced with a large number of smart dumb scholars. They are smart in a way that they have mastered their chosen fields of study in a way that arguably no other generation has. Dumb in a way that they fail to observe their knowledge from a holistic perspective, and they therefore make serious blunders technically, creatively, as well as ethically.

We live in a society that tries to skew everything into the right eye schools that favor the logical left brain. Thus the talk of social sciences… attempts to try and explain society using the scientific method.

But let us be critical in our thoughts for a moment, can this actually be done? Can we call sociology for example a science as we now allude? We have explored the development of physics in the previous chapter, and in order to understand what was happening, we had to understand some philosophical concepts; one of them was the concept of causality. Let us now expand this and now speak of the density of causality. Think of density as a concept of two objects of exactly the same size, but one is heavier than the other one, why, because it must be denser. So physics must have a high density of causality, since if you push a trolley it moves. And if we know a few variables such as how heavy the trolley is, how big the force at which we pushed it and how much friction the wheels experience, then we can calculate fairly accurately the path, speed and acceleration of the trolley.

By the time we have moved from physics through chemistry and on to biology, the density of causality also decreases. The variables are many and it becomes harder to determine what causes what and to replicate an experiment and to control conditions (one of the core principles of the scientific method is the ability to replicate experiments under controlled conditions). To overcome this, biologists repeat the experiment many times and then average out the results before analyzing them. A lot of work, but it is still science some argue, even thou there are over six hundred theories of ageing alone and some colleges simply get students to vote on which five theories to study due to time constraints (voting? starting to sound more political than scientific).

By the time one has moved from biology, through medicine onto psychology to sociology, the density of causality decreases even further. The variables involved in phenomena are many. And while we are still able to observe phenomena in the society, to attempt to explain them scientifically, one would need to reduce the society at least to the biological scale and study the billions of trillions of cells involved in the sample society whilst controlling the conditions of that society. And since no social scientists are busy with such an exercise, and we do not yet even have computers available for academic use that can collect, store and process such information, we must question those who explain society and pass it off as science. For they give us the impression that they have some definite knowledge of the processes of all societies at any given space or time, and that this is scientific, that this is somewhat built in to nature. And that is a lie. The social sciences therefore in this respect (and only in this respect to be respectful) are comparable to the pseudo-sciences.

Social scientists can today, if they really want to, prove what they want to prove, fit some graphs into it, make it look all scientific, but really the so called research is tainted by the biases of the researcher and of the society itself. This is not to say that we must stop the attempt to explain society quantitatively using numbers, we must always try, and so far social scientists have been very successful in answering the what about society in this way, but not the why. For that, for now, we must rely on qualitative methods. Sociology therefore is still very much an art and only a tiny bit scientific for now… and there is nothing wrong with that for as long as we acknowledge it.

Africans, we must recognize that the societies we reside in are far more evolved than even the bodies we inhabit. One example of this is the theory that suggests that the reason so many people are lactose intolerant is because we only started farming livestock and consuming dairy products as recently as about fifteen thousand years ago during the agricultural revolution; so our bodies still don't yet know what this dairy thing we are feeding it is. But if we think that is astounding, there are even more bizarre theories about how 'backward' our bodies are compared to our society. We once knew a doctor who for years tried to figure out why men always wet their pants with the few drops of urine that is left over every time they pee. When he figured it out, he had formulated a theory; that the reason some drops of urine were always left over is because there is a nerve reflex that causes this to happen because men touch their members when they pee. He experimented and found that when a male does not touch their member at all, then no urine is left behind. And since the only reason men touch their members when they pee is because they wear pants, he concluded that our bodies are not even yet used to the fact that we wear clothes… that evolutionary speaking, our bodies still assume that we are walking around naked, we stop, pee, and continue walking without touching anything, like every other mammal.

This perceived backwardness of our bodies is indeed scary to us, for something deep inside us tells us that we are not just animals… that we are in fact that and so much more. And so, as a reaction, a rebellion of sort, we deny the animal aspects of ourselves altogether. The more sophisticated the society we reside in, the more we frown upon actions that remind us of our animal aspect. Animals eat, and we eat too, so then we have all kinds of etiquettes with respect to eating and we have coined such terms as gluttony. Animals have body odor, and so do we, so we hide ours behind layers of deodorants, aftershaves, colognes and perfumes. Think of all the things that humans do and animals also do and you will find that these things are taboo (or at least frowned upon) and this society expects you to do these things in private (if you cannot avoid doing these things at all to begin with). Even something as natural and widespread as breastfeeding a child whenever and wherever it is hungry is now frowned upon as inappropriate amongst people of some societies.

And so, through this denial, we have gone on to do great things. We have denied our most basic urges to discover that we are in fact capable of so much more. How we can trick the forces of nature and create these completely artificial systems we call modern society is a uniquely human trait which we are so boastful and so proud of. According to us, there is absolutely nothing more amazing than us, and we use the societies we have built as the proof of this.

But Africans, we must be aware that in spite of our achievements, there are major flaws in the societies we have built. One example, whether scientists and politicians agree or disagree about the theories surrounding this, one cannot deny that a lot of the things we do to our environment since adopting the hydrocarbon based economy we have today are simply dirty. And as common sense would tell us, dirtiness goes against life and promotes death. Therefore, if we continue to be so dirty, we might create a situation in which we seriously compromise the health of the biosphere and thus in turn compromise our own health. The sickness in the biosphere is in fact a sickness in our society. When all living creatures, even the most basic single cell organisms, behave in such a way as to preserve and even sustainably propagate themselves, we must agree that for us to behave in a way in which we knowingly destroy ourselves is uncharacteristic of anything that is alive, healthy and striving; it is in fact a pathology on our part, a serious sickness.

Know Africans, that the root of the illness of our society can be traced back to us insisting on separating ourselves from nature. Our shortcomings are rooted in how we speak of nature as if we are not part of it. Through our trickery and mastery of nature, in our abilities to manipulate nature, we have somehow convinced ourselves that we are separate from nature. That there is nature and then there is us. And while we did this, we did not even know we are doing this. It was through the reductionist approach that we did this, for to master nature we had to reduce our understanding of it into forms that we can understand, and we had to step outside of nature and assume the position of the observer. But now we must, Africans, return to nature.

Without discarding the wonderful things we discovered since stepping out of nature; retaining all of our knowledge, creativity and technology, we must return the society back to nature without giving up the independence of being free from the harsh elements of nature. For nature, Africans, is the socket from which the batteries of society must be charged from. In this way, without a regression in society, we will create a future society that has been cured from the temporal illness our society had to experience while it morphed. When we model society around nature, when we embrace ourselves in these models as natural phenomena, then we can begin a renegotiation with nature; we renew diplomatic ties so to say. Then we allow ourselves to be tamed by nature as we continue to tame it. Then the relationship between society and nature will be symbiotic, mutually beneficial. In fact, nature and society will once again be one in the same, but this time at a much higher octave.

On the Physical Part 2

Newton's law of universal gravitation, although it worked reasonably well for the purposes of the times and certainly for most applications here on earth, did violate the first principle of mechanical theory; for it suggested that objects that were very far away from each other were indeed affecting each other. It became necessary to start thinking of many imaginary connections that were doing the pulling, and thus the idea of fields started to gain ground. The gravitational field, although we cannot see it, gave the mechanists a satisfactory explanation that perhaps there was some pulling and tugging happening in realms beyond our senses.

The field idea would continue when Gauss formulated a theory which explains how things spread out, the theory of divergence. This theory gave a mathematical explanation to such things as a fountain of water spreading out from a single source, and when reversed, the drainage of water in a sink when a stopper was pulled out. Gauss would then use this mathematics to study electricity. He found that a positive electric charge formed an electric field fountain and a negative electric charge formed an electric field sink, that opposite charges attract and similar charges repel, which was different from gravity which always attracts; this came to be known as Gauss's Law. Soon Gauss's Law of Magnetism was formulated, which suggested that unlike electric charges which can exist in monopoles, meaning that one can find either a positive or negative electric charge in nature all alone, magnets only exist in dipoles. This means that the positive and negative poles of a magnet are always in pairs, you cannot find one without the other, and if you cut a magnet in half, the magnetic fields in both halves would rearrange themselves so that there are negative and positive magnetic poles on both pieces.

Ampere and Faraday, at almost the same time period and from different labs would observe that there is some link between electricity and magnetism. The one found that a changing electric field produced a magnetic field while the other found that a changing magnetic field produced an electric field.

Maxwell would bring together the four laws, namely Gauss's Law, Gauss's Law of Magnetism, Faraday's Law and Ampere's Law, which together were to become known as Maxwell's Equations and which formally unified the electric field and the magnetic field into the electro-magnetic field. One could now speak of an electromagnetic wave, where the electric aspect of the wave was orthogonal (at 90 degrees) to the magnetic aspect, in other words, if the electric aspect of the wave is horizontal then the magnetic aspect would be vertical when both would be traveling forward.

Maxwell's work was a dream for the science fiction novelist, for it suggested that such things as mobile phones were theoretically possible. Today we take wireless communication for granted, but if people from Maxwell's time were to see us, they would think we are a society of witches and wizards who were engaging in pure sorcery. For the scientists, this was the end of the classical era of physics. One scientist even boldly suggested that physicist now knew everything there is to know about physics, and that the new work for physicists was not discovery, but to become more accurate in what was already known. But the issue of light was still a problem, and solving this problem would lead to what we now call modern physics.

Newton had studied light during his time. He suggested that light is a very small particle. But no matter how much he tried to get the particle model of light to work, it could never explain why light bends when moving from one medium to the next, say from air to glass; a phenomenon known as refraction. Other physicist had suggested that light was in fact a wave, like how sound was, but they were shut down quickly by the scientific community, because going against Newton was blasphemous in the church of science back in those days. In the turn of the 19th century, a scientist called Young showed that light does indeed consist of waves when he shined a light on a surface with two holes on it and a wave pattern appeared on a screen behind. But if light was a wave, it would need a medium, like how sound waves move through air. So scientists of that time suggested that there was something out there, which we cannot touch, we cannot see, we cannot smell and we cannot taste, which exists solely for the purpose so that light can move through it… they called this the ether.

Problems with this ether is that light was moving through it very fast, so it must be hard, but we cannot observe light slowing down due to rubbing against this ether, so it must be soft, and how can something be hard and soft at the same time? So on top of the fact that this ether was motionless, invisible, odorless and tasteless, this ether was also hard and soft simultaneously, a logical impossibility, and scientists began to accept that this ether was farfetched and most probably did not exist. This is another reason Maxwell's electromagnetic model was so important, because if electricity causes magnetism which causes electricity which in turn causes magnetism and so on, there was no need for this ether, for these electromagnetic waves could propagate themselves in this very way and could thus move in empty space. When these waves were shown to travel at the speed of light, it was then suggested that light could be a kind of electromagnetic wave.

But there were still problems with light. The first problem; scientists observed that if one person had a torch and was standing still and the other person had a torch and was inside a fast car, both lights from both torches would be the same speed. This breaks the laws of classical physics and common sense because surely the light from a moving source should be faster. The second problem with light was to be called the 'black body radiation and ultraviolet catastrophe', basically according to classical physics, a piece of burning coal was not supposed to just glow red, it should also glow blue even at fairly low temperatures. Solving these two problems was to lead to the formation of two branches of modern physics, relativistic physics and quantum physics; Einstein would be essential to both branches. Solving these problems would require scientists to do away with the mechanical model and with common sense; there was no longer a space for such in cutting edge physics.

Einstein was looking at himself in a mirror, when he started thinking, since the image on the mirror is in fact just light travelling from his face, to the mirror and back towards his eye, if he started running at the speed of light and since observations had shown that the speed of light does not increase even if the speed of the source of that light was increasing, would he still be able to see himself on the mirror? This line of thinking would lead him towards relativistic thought processes which were started by Galileo. Basically, when one drops a rock, we tend to think of the rock accelerating down towards the earth. But the mathematics is just as valid if you think of the very same situation but then the rock remains where it is and it is the earth which accelerates up towards the rock. To measure the speed of light, one needs a ruler and a clock (since speed is just length per time). Einstein, in his special theory of relativity, suggested that because person A running slowly with a ruler and a clock, and person B running fast with a ruler and a clock, still measured the same speed of light, perhaps it is the ruler that becomes shorter the faster you run, allowing the speed of light measurements to remain the same. Perhaps it is the clock which slows down the faster one goes. Further, the theory showed that when objects travelled very fast, objects became heavier. And so mass was nothing but just concentration of energy. This was represented in the famous formula $E=mc^2$, which suggested that even a tiny piece of mass has a lot of energy stored in it, this was all rather weird but was demonstrated to be true some forty years later with the catastrophic atomic bomb. But the initial resistance to Einstein's theory was understandable, for it suggested that if a pair of twins were born on the same day, grew up together and one twin travelled the universe at speeds approaching the speed of light and then came back, the twin that left would be an old man while the other one would be younger than the one that left because they have experienced time differently.

It was Einstein's desire to expand his Special Relativity theory to include not just uniform motion, but also acceleration, such as the angular acceleration which allows the earth to continue circling around the sun. Besides the rebelliousness against mechanical thought processes, the mathematics, specifically the geometry which was taking place at the time was also in a rebellion. Mathematicians were for the first time courageous enough to commit the blasphemous sin of questioning some of the ten assumptions of one of the church of mathematics undisputed gods, Euclid. For example, Euclid had said that if there is a point next to a straight line, then there is only one line which could be drawn which goes through this point and is parallel to the first line. But, a mathematician suggested that there were infinitely many lines that could be drawn through this point which would be parallel to the first line, and the mathematics was still logical and it worked even though this goes against common sense. Another mathematician came and said there was no line that could be drawn through this point which would be parallel to the first line, and guess what, that mathematics was still logical and it still worked. The geometries formulated from these new assumptions would come to be known as non-Euclidian geometry.

Applying this new mathematics, Einstein formulated his expanded theory, General Relativity, which suggested that space and time were one, what he called the space-time continuum. This theory produced very accurate results. For example, one could think of space-time as a fabric and a mass would then stretch the space-time fabric into a vortex like dent, which would then allow the earth to be caught up in an orbit around the sun the same way a piece of rice left over in the sink after washing dishes starts moving in a circle as you drain the water out of the sink, because the Sun is so heavy that it creates this dent in the space time fabric. General Relativity gave even more accurate results than Newton's Universal Gravitation, but the implications of it were absurd. For space-time suggested that the shortest distance between A and B was no longer the length of a straight line between A and B, but was in fact zero, because space-time can be bent so that A and B kiss each other and such things as teleportation were theoretically possible (like in those movies where one walks through a portal and is instantly transported elsewhere). Further, it suggested that just as one can move forward and backwards in space, one could also move forward and backwards in time (like in the Terminator movies).

Max Planck, in an attempt to explain blackbody radiation and the ultraviolet catastrophe suggested that light was an electromagnetic wave, which carried its energy in packets (quanta) which would be later called photons. Einstein, while attempting to explain another problem with light, the photoelectric effect, did so by assuming that Planck was correct, that light sometimes behaved like a wave and sometimes like a particle. The solution for the photoelectric effect is the science which would lead to today's solar panels and earned Einstein the Nobel Prize in 1921 which was only handed to him in 1922 due to disagreements within the church of science on whether he deserved it or not. Of course theories still had to be formulated on how something could behave like a particle sometimes and behave like a wave sometimes.

Heisenberg's quantum theory of uncertainty was to form one of the first popular branches of quantum physics. Heisenberg observed that the more one knows about how fast a particle was going the less one knows about where that particle is, and the more one knows about where the particle is the less one knows about how fast it was going. Therefore, one has to choose what information they wish to know more about, and accept that by knowing more about that then they knew less about other things. Further, Heisenberg made a grid and shot particles at it. But before he did, he asked other scientists to predict where on the grid the particles would occur, and the particles often times seemed to occur where the scientists had predicted. Heisenberg concluded that experimentation was flawed because even the act of measuring somehow changes that which is being measured. Things were just… uncertain.

This theory of uncertainty shook science at its roots, for it challenged determinism. Here was a theory which was growing in popularity and which suggested that an exact solution to the problems of science could not be determined, instead many solutions were possible, each solution with a probability that it may or may not occur. Einstein, now an old man and as absurd as his own theories were when he was a young man, dismissed these quantum theories when he famously said, "God does not play dice," referring to the links that probability theories have to gambling. Heisenberg, when he himself was an old man was asked about how his quantum theories became popular and practiced by so many young scientists, he answered that scientific theories do not become popular; rather the previous generations of scientists who oppose the theories get old and die.

There are other quantum theories from Heisenberg's time by other scientists which are only now becoming popular, which give similar results to Heisenberg's theories mathematically, but without the need for uncertainty. It is believed that the reason these quantum theories were dismissed at first is because they have philosophical implications that are far more absurd, and it was just easier for us to comprehend uncertainty than to try comprehending some of this other stuff. For example, some of these theories suggested that point non-locality is a real thing. Point non-locality suggests that if two things were associated with each other, then they were separated, making changes to one thing automatically makes changes to the other thing too instantaneously. This has now been proven to be possible in an experiment with subatomic particles.

In today's physics, there are four known force fields; gravity, electromagnetism, the strong force (which keeps the protons in an atom together despite the fact that they are all positive and should repel each other according to Gauss's Law) and the weak force (which is responsible for radioactive decay and has led to technologies such as carbon dating). Many attempts have been made to unify these forces, in the same way Maxwell unified electricity and magnetism and closed a chapter in the history of science. Some attempts are just overly complicated, like string theory which assumes eleven dimensions just to make the mathematics work… this approach is highly unlikely because it complicates things and what we know about nature is that it tends to offer very simple elegant solutions for the most fundamental of truths. Other attempts have only managed to unify some and not all of the force fields.

This problem of unifying the forces is known as the holy grail of mathematics and physics, or just toe (short for the 'theory of everything') or gut (grand unified theory). There are many such theories, but by far the most far reaching (and thus controversial) of these theories of everything is GAGUT (God Almighty's Grand Unified Theory) which was published by Prof Gabriel Oyibo in 1990. From just the name of the professor and the name that he decided to name the theory, one can see the controversy. Firstly, to name a scientific theory God Almighty's theory is an unforgivable sin in the scientific community (the church of science) who many of their members feel it is their God given mission to destroy the idea of God in the first place. So Prof Oyibo is a scientist, which makes the religious fundamentalists angry, but he sees no conflict between science and the idea of God, which makes the scientists angry, basically everyone is angry at Prof Oyibo. Secondly, Prof Oyibo is an African, and the global society was built on the colonial ideas that Africans and other indigenous peoples were eugenically inferior, so giving the torch of genius (the same torch which was held by Newton and Einstein) to an African is a big no for the church of science (the scientific community).

Funny enough, the biggest opposition for GAGUT has come from other Africans, those who do not even have the mathematical or scientific background to even understand or challenge the theory scientifically, never mind offering a better more refined solution themselves. At first, they tried to attack the professor's credentials, but they soon realized that this would not work since Prof Oyibo is a well decorated scientist who has done work for institutions that his critics see as credible scientific bodies (such as NASA). Next, they argue the fact that a Harvard, Oxford, Cambridge or Yale, although their scholars are studying GAGUT, have not come out and hailed GAGUT as the solution to the long awaited problem of unifying the force fields. So basically, this argument is rooted in colonial and slave thinking that for an African to be right, he/she must be verified, validated and approved by Europeans; which the Europeans will never do (until it is in their own interest to do so). Sadly, even those who accept GAGUT do so as blindly as those who oppose it, and as a scientist, Prof Oyibo does not approve of this either. Now we have spoken about many scientific theories in this work, and we have done so not as experts but as laymen and have done it in such a way that even a teenager can understand. For the sake of completion, we shall do the same with GAGUT.

Oyibo suggests the mathematical equation $G_{ij,j}=0$ as the most fundamental equation, where (G) is everything in existence (or God), (i) is the material and (j) is space-time. What this means in simple language is that God (or everything/the omnipresence) in the material and space-time dimensions does not change. In other words, this is a conservation theory (such as the energy conservation theory which states that energy cannot be created or destroyed, but is simply transformed from one form to another). Oyibo's theory is said to be consistent with other physical theories (such as $E=mc^2$) and not only does it unify all four known force fields with each other, it also unifies them with other force fields which have not yet been discovered. It is able to do this because GAGUT assumes a bird's eye view and it looks at the problem from an elevated position (as Einstein said, we cannot solve the problems we face at the same level of thinking as when we created them). GAGUT has solved many unanswered problems posed by such mathematicians as Riemann (who himself was a pioneering mathematician who challenged Euclid's geometry to form his own) and in chemistry GAGUT seems to suggest that there is only one element, hydrogen, and that all the other elements are compounds of this element as have been proven by nuclear fission.

There are few people in the world that understand how to derive or use GAGUT; Prof Oyibo is very happy in his lectures when he encounters such people who ask him hard scientific questions which he answers with confidence and one can see from the facial expression of those who pose the questions that they are indeed satisfied with the answers, one can see this even from the lack of follow up questions. But every now and again a lawyer, politician or tabloid journalist tries to deteriorate the conversation into personal slurs and insults and courtroom tricks of diverting the conversation away from the mathematics and science and framing the issue into what they want it to be. In what has been now almost three decades, there is yet to be a mathematical paper that disproves Professor Oyibo's God Almighty Grand Unified Theorem.

Some argue that this undue scrutiny is justified since Galileo got the same scrutiny and was almost hanged just for presenting his theory; Einstein had the same scrutiny from the public right until the bombs dropped on Hiroshima and

Nagasaki cementing his findings as not just scientific mumbo jumbo, but something that is very real to the common folk.

Others argue that African scholars and universities should stop seeking validation from foreign journals and rating institutions and should rather concentrate on bringing forth the technology which GAGUT implies is possible, which would give Africa and the world unlimited amounts of clean renewable energy and do away with scarcity so that man can be free from toiling away as he always has and bring forth an age where the primary goal of man is the pursuit of truth, beauty and the meaning of life. But research, the way it is currently done, requires lots of funding; lots of funding requires the public purse and political will.

On the Politics

Africans, there is politics in everything, but politics is not everything. So when we speak of critical thinking and dogma, we are being political; for critical thinking encourages change (left wing politics) and dogma encourages things to be forever fixed (right wing politics). When we say that these subject matters are being brought to you by a layman, we are being very political. For the layman has been encouraged to shut up and not have an opinion, while the expert has been encouraged to monopolize the truth and therefore the expert is robbed of the basic human need to learn and the layman is robbed of the basic human need of expression. When we say that this layman is an African, we are being dangerously political… we are in fact pushing this work underground and into obscurity; for nothing truly African can exist in the mainstream… for in existence, two things rarely occupy the same space at the same time.

Know, Africans, that when the mainstream tells your history, it will be told as if your existence began with slavery and colonialism, and this will be done to serve the interest of those who control mainstream education worldwide. But then this very education will at the same time teach that the African is the first human on this planet with a history that goes as far back as two hundred thousand years in his current form. This is but the first contradiction that you shall find in mainstream education, strike one. Not that they don't know your history African they do. But they will not call it history; they will call it anthropology, the study of savages. This is despite the fact that they are mesmerized by the knowledge of your ancestors and would rather credit your ancestors' creations to fictitious ancient aliens rather than acknowledge the intellectual and creative capabilities that is in your DNA, that you have inherited and is your birth right, strike two. They will go on to say that their understanding of existence is superior to yours Africans, but then you will find out from observing your own languages that even such things as Einstein's space-time has been known by your ancestors for the longest time when you notice that the Nguni word for time is the exact same word for space, where time is objectified and space is personified. Strike three and out.

You must, Africans, be very careful when you create public policy. It will be tempting to use the many isms they teach in political courses at the universities. These isms are only good for analyzing things in hindsight, for intellectual arm wrestling and for dividing us. You see Africans, by the time an idea gets to the university, it is obsolete. This is why business school professors are not the top businessmen and their students are not taught how to be the owner of a top business, they are merely taught how to be the guardians. This too is true in politics and in public policy, the isms are simply useless. This is why we spent so much time going through physical and natural phenomena, these are the things you must use when modelling public policy.

Always be aware of the cycles and stages involved in your policies, like how Copernicus was aware of the cycles and orbits of the planets; then, like Kepler, use mathematics to determine the exact quantity of time involved in each cycle. Like Galileo, be very observant; observe other policies which might be cousins and even siblings of the policy you are creating. Observe the physical reality and the mental state of the public for which the policy is been designed. You can observe second hand data, but preferably, try to collect your own data, your own questionnaires and make your own spread sheets, so that when the public asks you your rationale in your decision making, you do not stutter, you tell them exactly what you thought you were doing. But even better than this, involve the public in every step of the policy design process, in this way, you protect yourself completely for when they come rioting at town hall, you do not hide but are able to face them and tell them to calm down and that they are in fact the creators of the policy and they are responsible for its failures and successes, that they are owners and that you are merely the guardian of the policy.

In implementing public policy, make use of Newton's principles of motion. Firstly, be aware of the energy required to get things moving in the first place, for projects that have not gotten off the ground are most reluctant to catch on steam. If an outdated policy which was already being implemented exist, then use the momentum of that project and concentrate only on diverting the direction of the project to be in line with new policy… this will preserve energy so that you might use it elsewhere. Remember, Africans, that your actions are directly linked to how things are going to change, so if you find yourself behind a certain policy, then push, if you find yourself standing in front of a policy, then pull. But to be constantly a pusher or constantly a puller as we have observed in governing and opposition politics respectively has to be counterproductive. That is why, always be aware of the opposition reactions that will attempt to halt the progress, development and implementation of your public policies.

In getting elected and staying elected, make use of Gauss principles of divergence, electricity and magnetism. By staying in touch with the people, you are always aware which sentiments are sprouting and are about to spread like a fountain and you are also aware of the source; you are aware which sentiments are sinking and going out of fashion and you are aware of the reason and the source of the discontentment. Understand, Africans, that the human mind is electric in nature, and the human heart is magnetic in nature, it is therefore just as important to relate to the people both intellectually and passionately. For it is the mind connection that will get people on your side, if they agree with what you are saying; but it is their feelings that will give them the passion to get up and go vote. But remember, African, that the realms of politics are orthogonal (perpendicular) to the realms of physics. So while Gauss's laws of the mind and heart still apply, the directions are opposite... in the physical realms opposites attract but in the social and political realms like attracts like. And remember the findings of Ampere, Faraday and Maxwell... that when people's minds change and so do their hearts, and when people's hearts change and so do their minds, and that the political machine is driven by and propelled by the consistency of these changes.

At the end of it all, politics is not an end in itself, but the means to an end. Politics is merely about the laws we put in place to attempt to control our social environments, our so called ecology. And we do this to set ourselves up to be in a position to extract and make use of the wealth which is in our ecology; we do this for the economic benefits.

On the Economy

We have discussed, Africans, how the social scientists try to pass off their models, their attempts at describing social phenomena, as natural law. None are as guilty as those who teach the social science of economics. None of the isms involved in economic study will emancipate the African economically.

At the same time, many who oppose the current economic disposition fail to offer a solution of their own. An example of this is the monetary system. Some say we must stop using money altogether but they do not offer a better way to conduct trade; those who do offer a better way, such as Pablo Fresco's resource based economy, do not offer practical solutions on how we are going to move from the monetary system to their system.

Be careful, Africans, of those who suggest that the solution is to destroy and then rebuild the current system, for this will take many generations and we who are alive today will never see the promised land, nor can we guarantee that our children will. The destroy and rebuild mentality is a mentality of anarchists, who fail to recognize that such a solution is a solution that will be fueled by the tears of the African mother, for when things change in nature, there is a period of transition and confusion and it is always gets darker before dawn.

No, Africans, the solution is not to destroy the current economic disposition, but to ignore it. We must, Africans, begin by pretending that the current global economy simply doesn't exist. If we choose to love it with all our hearts, if we choose to get rich or die trying, then we will get consumed by the current economic system. And since we have not yet discovered a way to excel economically and still maintain our humanity at the same time, we will ultimately be enslaved and destroyed by such a mentality.

If we choose to hate the current economic disposition with all of our hearts, then we are doomed and will experience many more generations living in poverty, slavery, wages and salary. The current economic system can only exist if we love it or if we hate it, it feeds off our love and hate energy; if however we are indifferent to it, then it cannot affect us and it cannot exist; it doesn't see us so let us not see it.

To give this strategy practicality, to move from pretending that it doesn't exist to it really not existing, this is the strategy you will follow, African.

Continue with your everyday activity, go to school, go to work, and continue looking for and creating employment.

Tighten your belt; Consume less things. All that glitters is not gold. A lot of the things you use, Africans, you can actually do without. The only products you really need are those products that feed your body, your mind and your soul.

Make a survey of these products in your community Africans. Rank these products in order of importance. Then make sure that these products are made within your community.

Consciously choose to use the products that are created within your community; yes they will be more expensive at first, this is because of an economic principle known as economies of scale, which states that the more one manufactures in bulk, the cheaper the product produced will be.

But, in the long run, using these locally sourced and produced products will empower the community and it will give the community livelihoods, which will improve all the social and economic indicators, the crime rate will go down, the unemployment rate will go down, there will be more money flowing in the community and it will flow through more hands, and every hand that it flows through will pocket a small percentage. By choosing to pay a little extra now for products that are made within your community, one will ultimately save more… because less will be spent on useless products such as security and insurance, these products will be obsolete.

We will become so good at making our things ourselves Africans, that we will catch the attention of other communities. They might want to join our communities or they might want to displace us to enjoy the fruits of our labor, they might even want to go to war due to the feelings of envy. So, when we become fully self-sufficient, and when we produce so much that there is a surplus, then we must simply give it away… for when we were still in nature, when we were still in the jungle, if you picked something up, you eventually had to throw it away to free up your hands, it made no sense to keep it. It might be tempting to trade our surplus for their products; we must, Africans, refrain from doing such, for we will then once again grow a dependency for their things and start regressing economically. If we like their things that much, then we must learn how to make them ourselves.

In short, Africans, we will create our own systems that are parallel to the current systems, and as our systems grow then the current system will become obsolete. This is because the current system is dependent on how we value it. If we stop valuing it, then everything in it, even its money will be worthless. If we stop valuing it, then the products that are produced by it will be worthless, no matter how much they market them to us.

Our economic emancipation, Africans, is dependent on us being the ones who add value to every single product we use at every single stage of the supply chain from the natural sources of the raw material to the finished products. Value is the only currency, but value doesn't exist in the physical realms, it exists only in the realms of the psyche.

On the Psychology

It is therefore of greatest importance, Africans, that we fully control all the socializing structures in our communities in order to free our psyche from the grips of other communities.

This will be resisted at all levels. For example, child services might decide to take our children away from us if we decide to take them out of the public schools when they teach our children lies so that they may hate themselves. So don't take your child out of the schools. But discuss with your child every single thing which is being taught. Teach your child the difference between the right answers to the questions of their assignments versus the answers they must actually right down in order for their teachers to give them the marks. Teach your kids never to oppose the teachers directly and in front of other children of other communities, for this will reveal their hand, and in a card game, one never reveals the hand they have been dealt. But rather, they must come home and do their own research, consult their brothers and sisters and other sources which have been vetted by the African conscious and intellectual community.

Do not switch off the television, or avoid the lies that the media will tell your kids so that they may hate themselves, Africans. Rather, teach your children to be critical of every single frame and every single word in the news and in their entertainment. This is until the African conscious community has its own news and its own media.

Teach your children, Africans, that the laws that were implemented in order to assist the mentally ill are the same laws that will be used against them when they become too much of an independent thinker. Teach them how even a criminal has more rights than a mental health patient; the criminal has the right to remain silence, the right to a phone call, the right to an attorney, the right to be charged within twenty four hours and if not charged, the right to be released and if not released, the right to sue. The mental health patient has no rights at all. He can be held for seventy two hours for 'observation' and thereafter a psychiatrist can decide to lock him up forever and ever without a trial, without the right to refuse treatment which is being forcefully drugged with poisons which will make them drug addicts forever and ever.

So it is essential African, that when we conduct our mental emancipation, we go about our business as 'normally' as possible. This will be extremely hard, ever seen a horror movie where an exorcism takes place? Ever seen a super hero movie, when they transform, how hard it is? That is how hard this is going to be and it is easier for those around you to simply label you as crazy and lock you up out of concern, love and ignorance of natural phenomena.

Lastly, Africans, have the mental strength to come back to 'normal' consciousness and free up other brothers and sisters that are still trapped in the matrix; this will only work if when you approach them you already look like what they aspire to be. Do not be forceful, many of them still love the matrix and will resent you for freeing them. But you too, Africans, must always be aware, that every freedom is a chain that imprisons you from an even greater freedom, this is a basic metaphysical law.

On the Metaphysics

When things transcend from a state of non-existence into existence, they start off very small in size that one might not see them, but they are very heavy due to the potential that is pregnant within them.

At first, they do not move, and then they start moving in straight lines and eventually they learn how to move in curves.

They learn to swim in the waters, and then they learn to fly in the sky, before they look as if they have disappeared back into non-existence, when in fact they are in labor, giving birth to everything that exist.

How? Well it first survives. Then it reproduces. Then it discovers wealth. Then it loves. Then it expresses itself. Then it knows itself. Then it unites with the all. Then it is at peace. And then it returns.

On the Religions

Of all the things said in this work, which seem to be bashing your religions, we respectfully apologize, Africans.

The religions of old are tried and tested and they have been known to work.

Problems arise when they try to convince you that you do not need to know why they work… you do need to know, Africans, for everything that hurts you, Africans, is rooted in ignorance.

All institutions tend to behave in such a way as to preserve themselves first. Eventually, everything they do will be in the name of self-preservation at all costs, even at the cost of the core principles of that institution.

It is easy to suggest that we put an expiry date on each and every institution to combat against this.

This is known to have detrimental effects, for it creates a vacuum; something must come and fill the void that is left over, and most of the time, that thing that comes is of lesser quality than what we were trying to get rid of. This is why people are walking out of the churches, temples and mosques due to things that they see that they do not like… only to find themselves consumed by emptiness and a moral void.

We must, Africans, not destroy institutions, but rather attempt to reform them. But this cannot be done from within them. Most systems are so big that when we try and reform them from within they end up reforming us. We must rather create new systems, and use the old ones as stepping stones and pedestals to hold the new ones up. When we do this, then the old systems, including the religions, will reform themselves.

Ultimately, when the religions become metaphysically consistent, psychologically beneficial, economically viable, politically compatible, scientifically correct and socially responsible… only then will any religion be fit to be practiced by us, Africans, and to be practiced religiously. For the religions, whichever one we choose to practice, will serve us, and not the other way around.

Conclusion

So if these words are by an African would it be safe to say then that they are for the Africans? More importantly, who are 'the Africans'?

There was a time when these questions were simple to answer; when one could open up an encyclopedia, consult a dictionary, visit the library and if one still couldn't find answers simply ask an elder, a clergy or whoever's claims one was willing to believe.

But the information age is upon us, with all its glory and sadness combined. Glory in the sense that the days where information is traded for monetary value or power or both are numbered, for soon all information will be available and will be free. But also sadness in the sense that, well two phenomena that were seen online that motivated the scripting of these words; very sad indeed.

The first is characterized by a guy who uploads arguments online, stressing why people should not believe the lies that scientists are telling us for surely the world is a flat disk. At first glance, one would think this fellow was just joking and uploads such an article for fun, until one reads on and gets shocked by the compelling evidence the guy provides to prove his argument. Then one gets worried because this fellow isn't joking, in this day in age, he truly believes the world is flat... Then one gets even more worried when one reads the public's comments... although most people are shocked and outraged by this fellow's post, there are actually a lot of people who side with him and post comments like, "I agree with ya 100%" or "I knew it, how can it be round anyway, I can't believe I bought that story for so long, my kids will be home schooled" and things of that nature. Few could have predicted that in the information age, with the volumes of quality and non-quality information alike, it becomes a task in itself to distinguish which is which. So just when humans were just about ready to switch off our brains and let computers do the hard thinking, we are now called upon to once again think... And think very critically.

To you, Africans, the earth is a dimensionless-sphere also known as a point if you are infinitely far away from it; it is a two dimension sphere also known as a disk if you are a flat earth enthusiast we just discussed or if you are a dog which chases its tail for it sees not depth; it is a circle if you project this disk into its one dimensional circumference and it is a straight line if you project the circle from an orthogonal view; it is a three dimensional sphere also known as simply a sphere or a ball if you are man; it is a fourth dimensional sphere also known as a hyper-sphere if you are a god; it is an n-sphere also known as the set of points in (n+1) dimensional space that are at distance (r) from a central point where (n) is any integer and (r) is any real number if you are God… to you African, the earth is all these things and more.

The second sad story we see online everyday are the wars of dogma in the Middle East. As Africans, we have serious problems of our own so we shouldn't really be bothered by all this, but we find ourselves caught in the middle because of the Judeo-Christian-Islamic ties which we inherited from colonial and slave masters, and the fact that a neighbor's stockpile of dirt will eventually spill over to your own yard.

Perhaps our kids, Africans, will be bothered when foreigners come to Africa again in the next wave of colonization, this time instead of sending the armies and the missionaries to shoot first and brainwash later, they will send in geneticists and lawyers who will prove scientifically in some international court that the foreigners are indeed of African descent and ancestry (who isn't?) and are therefore entitled to the control of the ecology of Africa.

And here lies the conundrum. How can one speak of critical thinking, logic and science without speaking of the dogma, ethics and values, when clearly one is used to breed the other and the other is used to prove the one? When this is understood, then there is no paradox at all because things just come together. The lines become blurred. Critical thinking and dogma merge and become one in the same. Then Africans all over the world, whoever dares to refer to themselves as such, are the Africans that this work was scripted for.